P9-ECZ-630

HEALING WATERS
The Pilgrimage to Lac Ste. Anne

For Mac Simon

The University of Alberta Press

HEALING WATERS

The Pilgrimage to Lac Ste. Anne

STEVE SIMON

Published by
The University of Alberta Press
Athabasca Hall
Edmonton, Alberta
Canada T6G 2E8

Printed in Canada   5 4 3 2 1

Photographs copyright © Steve Simon, 1995
Text by Steve Simon, copyright © The University of Alberta Press, 1995

ISBN 0-88864-277-6

Canadian Cataloguing in Publication Data

Simon, Steve, 1960–
    Healing waters

    Includes bibliographical references
    ISBN 0-88864-277-6

    1. Christian shrines—Alberta—Lac Ste. Anne. 2. Indians of North America—Alberta—Religion.
3. Christian pilgrims and pilgrimages—Alberta—Lac Ste. Anne. 4. Lac Ste. Anne (Alta.)
I. Title.
BX2321.L32S55 1995   263'.042'0899707123   C95-910659-6

All rights reserved.

No part of this publication may be produced, stored in a retrieval system, or transmitted in any forms or by any means, electronic, mechanical, photocopying, recording, or otherwise, without the prior permission of the copyright owner.

Color separations and film work by Elite Lithographers Co. Ltd., Edmonton, Alberta, Canada.

Printed and bound by Quality Color Press, Inc., Edmonton, Alberta, Canada.

Printed on recycled (10% post-consumer waste fiber, 50% recycled fiber), acid-free paper. ∞

COMMITTED TO THE DEVELOPMENT OF CULTURE AND THE ARTS

PREFACE

When I first arrived at Lac Ste. Anne the summer of 1988, I was captivated. I felt a positive spiritual energy that transcended any religious barriers. As a photographer, I was struck by the beauty of the people, both spiritual and physical; their kindness, generosity and warmth. I kept coming back.

These photographs did not start out to be a book, but were an attempt to capture the mystery and aura of the event. After talking to people and hearing their experiences of healing, I asked to record their words, preserving the stories that could someday be used in an exhibition of the work. After several years of making photographs and not seeing much published material on the pilgrimage, the idea of this book came about.

This book's purpose is not to be an anthropological study of the Lac Ste. Anne Pilgrimage, but to share with you the stories and images that generous people were so willing to share with me. The quotations accompanying the photographs were not necessarily spoken by the people pictured, but were chosen because they reflect the mood or content of the images beside which they appear.

The pilgrimage is a magical, spiritual place of great healing and harmony. A place that really seems to make a positive difference in people's lives, including mine.

AUGUSTANA UNIVERSITY COLLEGE LIBRARY

i

ACKNOWLEDGEMENTS

As with any big project, there are many people to thank. The people whose names and faces appear in this book were very generous with their time and thoughts and there would be no book without them. In particular, I'd like to thank the people of the Alexis First Nations, specifically, Francis Alexis, Adam Rain, Cecile Potts, Helen Letendre, Jean Alexis, Pearl Kootenay and Eugene Alexis.

Olive Dickason shared her wisdom with constructive suggestions. Father Jacques Johnson and the Oblate Order provided much needed advice, cooperation and feedback over the years. Hobbema Artist Alex Twins painted the beautiful murals that are included in several of the photographs.

University of Alberta Press editor Mary Mahoney-Robson, graphic designer Alan Brownoff, Phillipa Pawlyk in promotions and director Glenn Rollans made this final result much better than the rough version I brought to them.

For their help and encouragement I thank: Chief Johnsen Sewepegaham, Earle Waugh, Maggie Hodgson, Doreen Spence, Alice Charland, Michael Payne, David Young, Veronica Morin, Father Gaston Monmenier, Andrea Marrantz, Norma Gutteridge, Susan Cardinal, Raven Makkinnaw, Elizabeth

MacPherson, Father Alfred Groleau, the Alberta Beach Museum committee, Don Dutton, Barb Good, Jeffrey Black, the Edmonton Art Gallery, Karen Gagnon, Father Rene Fumoleau, Anne Anderson, Susan Berry, Sister Fernande Champagne, Cindy Gaudet, Scott McKeen, Pat Beuerlein, Wendell Phillips, Father Camille Piché, Ken Cowill, Darlene Willisko, Jenny Poon, the Poundmaker Nechi Center, Kathleen Hugessen, Patty Reksten, Denis Gauthier-Villon, Vi Trivett, Dave Smith, Jack and Ethel Gordon, Larry Towell, George Webber, Paul Van Peenen, Jules Richer, Ross Greer, Mitch and Trina Baum, Bert Crowfoot, Bob Chelmick, Andre Chitayat, Charlene Dobmeier, Lindsay Chrysler, Tom Mayenknecht and Ted Grant.

I would also like to thank the *Edmonton Journal* for their support, in particular, my friends and colleagues in the photo department: Shaughn Butts, Jim Cochrane, Bruce Edwards, Brian Gavriloff, Ed Kaiser, Rick MacWilliam, Judith Pacquin, Greg Southam, Larry Wong, Ian Scott, Ken Orr, Mike Pinder, Karen Sornberger, Colin Shaw, Cheryl Shoji, John Lucas, Steve Makris, Neil Smalian and Bryant Avery. Kodak Canada's Terry Holmes and Chuck Brown and Nikon Canada's Larry Frank also need to be mentioned. A grant from Western Canadian Publishers is gratefully acknowledged.

I am grateful to photographers and workshop leaders Sam Abell, Eugene Richards and Mary Ellen Mark, and to my fellow students, for their teachings and inspiration, and to sounding boards Randy Mark, Chris Schwarz, Teresa Simon, Frances Simon and Barb Musey. Thanks to all.

Steve Simon

ALFRED BILLETTE
DILLON

"I believe in the water because water is God to us, without water there is no life."

THE HEALING WATERS OF
LAC STE. ANNE

Every year, thousands of people make their way to the water. On a hot July day, a seemingly endless stream of buses, pick-up trucks, and cars with campers in tow bump down the dusty, gravel road that leads to Lac Ste. Anne in northwestern Alberta.

Grandmothers, many too weak to make it on their own, grasp rosary beads as they hold the arms of their children and slowly wade through the shallow water. Mothers and fathers with small children stand near shore and pray, the water gently and rhythmically lapping over their feet. There are many stories of people being healed here. These murky waters are said to have miraculous healing powers. This healing force is one reason thousands are drawn to this place. They come to be healed—physically, spiritually and emotionally.

Native people make the journey walking, many barefoot, as a means of self-sacrifice. Tradition is what calls some people to the lake, others come because of their religious beliefs. They socialize, spend time with relatives and renew old friendships. For this one week in July every year, a 40-acre Alberta shoreline is transformed into a magical tent city, the bright colours of tents and teepees dotting the meadow. On top of the open-air shrine, a neon cross emits a ghostly glow, symbolizing the long-standing presence of the Roman Catholic Church.

Whatever their reasons, the faithful have made a pilgrimage to Lac Ste. Anne for more than 100 summers, and for hundreds, perhaps thousands of years before that. Today, the annual pilgrimage to Lac Ste. Anne has become the largest Native gathering in Canada.[1]

But long before the missionaries first arrived to set up their church in 1843, the lake had been a traditional summer gathering place for the nomadic Native people. Life was everywhere. Fish were plentiful in the sparkling clear water. With an abundance of small animals and several varieties of berries carpeting the land, everything the people depended on for life was here. Ceremonies that celebrated life, including the sun dance and marriages, took place at the lake. People traded roots and herbs used for medicine and special stones needed for tools and arrowheads. It was a sacred lake, a power spot, a place of spiritual renewal. The lake was called "Manito Sakahigan" by the Cree who first came here,[2] meaning "Lake of the Spirit." The Alexis First Nations people who now live on the northwestern shore of the lake, call it "Wakāmne"[3] or "God's Lake."

It is unclear why the first priests who arrived at the lake renamed the water "Devil's Lake."[4] They may have misinterpreted the Cree meaning for "Lake of the Spirit" or perhaps they thought the spirit at the lake was evil. The water was often choppy and dangerous, prone to sudden and severe storms,[5] another possible reason for the "Devil" monicker.

In the Native oral tradition, many stories from long ago circulate among the people. Alexis First Nations band member Vernon Jones tells of a legend that explains the unpredictable waters.

There was a big monster that would appear in the lake. Because it moves in there, it is what caused the current. Only very few people saw it. Because of this they called it Devil's Lake. Ever since they blessed the lake and changed the name, there was no sighting of any kind of movement of the lake and it had become a very healing place for our First Nations people.[6]

By the mid-nineteenth century, there was competition among the Methodist, Anglican and Roman Catholic missionaries. In 1842, Father Jean-Baptiste Thibault, a determined diocesan priest, had already reconverted many Natives who had become Methodists to Catholicism.[7] While in Fort Edmonton, he heard of a lake with a thriving fishery that was also a gathering spot in advance of the annual buffalo hunts.[8]

The Catholic missionaries saw the site as central to the northern (Cree) and southern (Blackfoot) people, and the trail to the lake meant easier access to the roaming nations who travelled along this route. They also wanted some distance between themselves and a powerful and controlling Hudson's Bay Post in Edmonton. The lakeside location seemed ideal.

On September 8, 1843, Father Thibault established the first Catholic Mission in the Canadian Northwest at Devil's Lake. He renamed the lake "Lac Ste. Anne" after his patron saint, St. Anne, fulfilling a promise he made to her when he first arrived in the west in 1823.[9]

THE GRANDMOTHER SPIRIT

The naming of the lake after the mother of Mary, the grandmother of Jesus, proved to be auspicious. The grandmother is an important figure in Native culture. She is cherished, an intermediary between the ones that went ahead and the ones that are coming up, a link between the two realms. In the Cree language, St. Anne is referred to as "N'okkuminân,"[10] meaning, "our grandmother."

Father Jacques Johnson, one of eight Oblate Provincial Superiors[11] in Canada, has been pilgrimage director from 1986 to 1995. His religious order, the Missionary Oblates, have run the mission since 1856. He points out that, unbeknownst to the church at the time, the naming of the lake was appropriate because St. Anne's relationship to Jesus had meaning for the people:

> The reality of St. Anne as being the grandmother of Jesus is something that when I grew up did not exist. It was not until I became a priest that I heard that expression, St. Anne, the grandmother of Jesus. She was the mother of Mary, and we prayed to her because she was the mother of Mary. The First Nations people went one step further because in their culture the grandmother means so much. The grandmother is the most important member of the whole family, she is the one that raises the grandchildren and has the greatest influence on the grandchildren, even more so than the mother. She is respected and she is mourned the longest, and that special affection for the grandmother is something that, in a sense, is transferred to St. Anne. The connection being made has to do with the love and affection they have with their own grandmother. They related to St. Anne as the grandmother of Jesus.[12]

The connection between the grandmother and the ancestral world is another reason why Native culture looks at the grandmother and grandfather spirits with such high regard, according to Dr. Earle Waugh, author and religious studies professor, who has studied Native religions for more than 25 years:

> Grandmothers and grandfathers are … intermediary spirits; they are not in the body as we are but yet they are not spiritual powers without definition as in the ancestral world. So in the aurora borealis, you are really seeing all the spirits dancing in the other world and grandmother spirits are, so to speak, on the way there. They are helper spirits then. Your identity is linked with theirs in a tribal sense and your identity is the forward point of your whole ancestral line. What you want to do is keep this ancestral line going and the grandmother spirit wants you to do that." [13]

The high regard for the grandmother figure may have come from the significant role she played in the survival of early tribal societies, according to historian Dr. Olive Dickason, who has lectured and written extensively on Canada's First Nations people. Grandmothers and mothers were extremely important as food providers. Many archaeological and standard historical references on early hunting and gathering societies mention the importance of the hunters, because hunters left a recognizable debris.

> But the grandmothers were perhaps more important. The more that scholars began to understand early diets, the more they realized that meat was important, but it was not the only object in the diet. Plants were extremely important and it was grandmother and mother who went out and gathered the plants and roots. There are some estimates that even in hunting and gathering societies, plants made up as much as 75 per cent of the diet. So the grandmother was a major food provider.[14]

NATIVE SPIRITUALITY AND CATHOLICISM

Early colonization occurred in areas of significance to Native people, in places like Manito Sakahigan. The early missionaries realized that these places would be good bases to work from. They saw similarities in their traditions and aboriginal ones. Manito Sakahigan was God's lake, a healing lake. Because respect is perhaps the one value that underlies all Native culture, it is not surprising that the Native people respected the religious beliefs of the newcomers. Dr. Dickason believes Native people did not see the spirit world as being an exclusive one:

It was not just inhabited by Christian deities or by Muslim deities or Indian deities, there were all kinds of spirits floating around. When you were with the whites, you would accept the white gods because that was appropriate under the circumstances. But when you were in your hunting camp or in your own world, you turn to the hunting Gods or the "Keepers of the Game" for whom the Catholics have no provision for. So if you wanted to get game, getting in touch with a spirit, dreaming, was important. You got in touch with the appropriate spirits, so you could be lead to the proper places. The Catholics would say it was heresy. Native beliefs do not see any reason why the two can not operate side by side.[15]

Helen Letendre, an elder living on the Alexis First Nations Reserve, remembers clearly what her grandmother told her about the lake:

She heard these stories from her grandmother or her mom. When the mission came, she used to tell me, maybe the priests and the spiritual people know that it's something that's holy there, in Lac Ste. Anne. All these different kinds of people, all of them are not Catholic, they come from all over the place. They know it is special.[16]

Little Red River Cree Nation Chief Johnsen Sewepegaham believes that there can be a melding of Native tradition and Roman Catholicism:

The cross and the pipe can come together, it's up to the people to accept that. Of course, there are a lot of people out there who will tell us otherwise. People have told me otherwise. They say that this is Indian spirituality and this is White space; the two cannot mix.

My feeling to that is, God is one and the same, why can't the two mix? In my opinion, I am not praying to a different God. Even though other people will say, "Well, that is a White man's God." Well, to me, there is no such thing as a White man's God.

God is God. He is the king of the whole universe, the one that controls everything. For whatever purpose He created us in different nationalities or different languages, for whatever reasons He had. That was His way. I'm not going to question that. People can come together in a neutral ground and pray, to the same God that they've always prayed to.

The water is blessed with the name of Jesus. Jesus is a neutral person that would help anybody and everybody out there asking for help. It doesn't matter what religion, what nationality you are, everything is the same with God. I could be standing next to a person from the Blood tribe, for example, or the Blackfoot people and they are all your friends. They are asking for the same thing that you are asking for and you pray for them. When people go and they pray there, they pray for everybody that is asking for help.[17]

Veronica Morin, an Elder from the Enoch Reserve, first came to the pilgrimage when she was a four-year-old. She says Native people have come back for 60 or 70 years, because the lake was sacred even before the missionaries arrived.

I know Indian teachings and I know church teachings, and what the old people said to us, especially the ones like our grandmothers who were over one hundred, they said if you can't follow your own culture, if you can't pray in your own culture, at least pray within the church, someplace, pray. It means that you recognize the Creator has the supreme power. They prayed under the Catholic religion, but it doesn't matter where you pray and how you pray as long as you do.[18]

Father Jacques Johnson says that many aboriginal people embraced Christianity and Catholicism because they could relate to its ceremonies and variety of symbols:

The basic elements for the sweat lodge are water, stone or earth, air and fire, and these are found in the Catholic Church. The water of baptism, the stone and the altar that contains the relics of saints. Fire: candles and the incense that we have and their sweetgrass. Even the world of spirits, in everlasting life, the souls live on.

The Indian people speak of spirit helpers. They have their own in their own tradition. I see that there's a meeting place somewhere. The Church down the road may be truly enriched by discovering that there is a reality there of the spirit helpers who are most akin to what we call the guardian angels, expressed in their culture through the animal helpers. The Church does not come to evangelize only, but also to be evangelized. I look at Lac Ste. Anne and that reality of people of different tribes and nations coming together is very fundamental there. It's open to all people and all backgrounds. It's a place where people can feel comfortable. It's a safe place people tell me.[19]

HEALING

Perhaps the aspect of the pilgrimage that is most common between the two cultures is healing. Almost everyone you talk to, if they have not been healed personally, know someone who has. The idea of Lac Ste. Anne as a place of healing was noted at the first pilgrimage in 1889. Seventeen different instances of cures or healings are found in the *Codex historicus*, a diary written in French by a priest, recording the affairs of the mission as they pertained to the Oblate Order. The following excerpts were documented at pilgrimages between 1889–1891.

1) A person by the name of Paquet is cured of a lung ailment which has lasted for fifteen months and which has reduced him to utter weakness.

2) Rose Whelan, forever sickly, now is much stronger and improving daily. …
4) John Perreault, 8 years old, son of Adolphe Perreault, suddenly recalled from what seemed to be the very threshold of death. …
12) Mrs. Baptiste Courtepatte whose serious and long standing limp disappears. …
15) Jean Baptiste Nipissing, a man from the Mountains, who has been carried into the church because he cannot go three steps without excessive pain even if he uses a cane, leaves this stick as an ex-voto after the mass he attends. He walks out on his own power and with a firm step.[20]

James Medford, a paramedic who has worked at Lac Ste. Anne during the pilgrimage, has heard many stories about the healing properties of the lake:

Talking to some of the older people here, I think there's something to it. One elderly lady said when she was in her teens she was in the sanitarium in Edmonton for tuberculosis. She escaped one weekend and walked out here barefoot. When she went back to the sanitarium when the weekend was over, the tuberculosis lesions on her legs were healed and gone and she was released. Lesions disappearing over a weekend, it doesn't happen. I mean the obvious thing everybody thinks it's all psychosomatic. You feel good, you get cured. I just don't know.[21]

THE WATER

People come to the water to bathe, and pray. They collect the murky water of Lac Ste. Anne in milk jugs, pop bottles and gas containers to use throughout the year and to give to those who could not make it to the lake. For these people the water is the healing agent. A powerful symbol in Catholicism, water that is blessed by priests becomes holy, and is used to cleanse and baptize.[22] For Natives, it is the fourth power of creation, the "blood of the land."

Chief Johnsen Sewepegaham believes in the healing power of the water.

As a Native person I believe that water has always been sacred. When the water's blessed through prayer and through faith, of course, people can be healed. God can use the water to heal the people. I don't believe that the water itself would necessarily have that power. I believe that God, the Creator, is the one that puts the healing power in that water for the people to be healed spiritually and physically both, that's how I believe in it.

Because we Native people believe that God has the authority and power to use any element on earth to heal people because He's the Creator. He created everything, so with us, everything has a physical and a spiritual purpose. The herbs out there have different purposes, different ways of healing people. Water is one of the main elements for living. If we didn't have water, we don't live. Likewise spiritually, we believe it has the same purpose.[23]

The importance of water to the Native culture can be traced back to myths and legends surrounding the beginning of creation, says Dr. Waugh:

The mythic comprehension among the Cree people, for example, that the world was a huge ocean in which Creator was in some kind of raft and He sends down a beaver or some little animal to get earth from the bottom of the ocean. The animal dies getting a bit of earth under his fingernails and he comes up to the surface and then Creator takes that earth from under his fingernails and that is where the land comes from. So water is a primal substance.

It is also mythic in the sense that in some myths of origin, the ancestor figure opens his veins and dies and becomes the earth. This is a Sioux tra- dition. He opens his veins and his veins become the water on the earth. His flesh becomes the earth.

So in effect the very spiritual force of the Creator is present in water. This, ceremonially, takes on importance in the sun dance, where water is utilized as a holy sacrament or in the sweat lodge where water is the ingredient that is turned to steam, becoming a means of communication with the other world. It is a purifying agent. So, entering into the water not in the spiritual sense as a kind of symbolic washing away, but a sense of returning to origins before the world came. By going into the water with this spiritual power, it is a kind of return to spiritual sources.

I think in Lac Ste. Anne's case the water was the focal point for where the spirits were. But as this has developed, the whole area became sacred because it was a spiritual place. I would say that the water is numinous, but by virtue of the water being numinous the whole area is held to be cordoned off by that numinosity.[24]

During the Native sweat lodge, the healer will dip a branch with leaves or a stick in water and sprinkle it on the hot rocks. The resulting blast of steam involves the participants and assists in the healing, according to anthropologist Dr. David E. Young who has studied health and healing among Native cultures for 10 years as director of the Centre for the Cross-Cultural Study of Health and Healing:

One healer refers to this as a soup. A Dakota healer refers to it as "the breath of the grandfather." So this energy—the rocks are grandfathers and have been there from the beginning, and they're heated and when the water then is sprinkled on them, the heat from the rocks is transformed into the steam which becomes the healing agent.[25]

"Water as healing agent is also symbolized by the spirit hovering over the water, bringing life to the world," says Father Johnson:

The connection of water and spirit, that primeval element, water—life giving. The theme of water is connected, not only with material life but spiritual life. It is also connected with healing.

Water is so common. In itself, it cannot accomplish anything unless there is a special element of faith, whereby it gathers a new momentum that brings people further in their lives and their growth. So the priest that blesses the water will always insist in the connection between the water and baptism, because this is when we become one with Christ. This is when we are born again as spiritual people.[26]

SPIRITS AND DREAMS

An archaeological survey of the lake in 1979 found evidence of people inhabiting the area before contact with Europeans.[27] In 1994, archeologists estimated the remnants of a stone arrowhead or knife found at the site to be 5,000 to 6,000 years old.[28] Native stories suggest the lake has always been spirit-empowered. The sacred nature of contact with the spirit world would probably transcend any tribal distinctions, so a range of nations would gather here. Those who harbored hostilities towards each other would set them aside when they shared the commonalty of the sacred space.[29] Father Johnson has heard this story:

I am told that before the missionaries came that this was a sacred lake, and that Indian people would come in pilgrimage to pray, to bathe in the water and to be purified.

Even at the time when there were wars between different tribes, if the people of an enemy tribe would go to the lake, then they would be free to go, unmolested, to that area. It was a holy thing that they were doing and people respected that.[30]

These sacred places, or "power spots" as they are sometimes referred to, are ancient. In Native culture, often these are places one goes on a vision quest. Native healers have long traveled to these power centres to get recharged. Dr. Young says that Native people take a more spiritual view when it comes to identifying power spots, but that some cultures, the Chinese for example, take a more systematic approach to locating power spots:

Usually there is water, usually there is something overlooking the water and there is a particular shape of the land that is overlooking the water and so forth. They feel it has to do with magnetic fields that are set up by particular configuration of these physical things. So I don't think you can rule out the possibility that there might be certain spots that maybe adjust energies in your body in some way. There is a lot of Chinese medicine based on this. They feel there are certain spots that help align energy.[31]

This energy can be expressed in dreams and visions, an important part of Native culture. The dream world exists in the unconscious and is a part of the real world in Native tradition. Dreams are sacred, and they may come from the mind itself or from spirits outside the mind, to be interpreted and used to help guide oneself through everyday life.[32] Aboriginal traditions speak of journeying to the spirit world for enlightenment or for spiritual power. This journey or pilgrimage as a means of finding truth is often manifested through dreams or visions.[33]

"I know of a lot of people that have had visions or dreams and I personally have had some myself," says Chief Johnsen Sewepegaham:

Sometimes when I'm asked to talk at Lac Ste. Anne I might share some of those visions, but it is not very often. Different tribes have different ways of conducting their affairs. For us, we are very careful about how we go about talking about the visions that we have.

One main reason why I continue to go back to Lac Ste. Anne is that I've had those spiritual dreams or visions that were realistic.

The area where the confessional is, it is built like a teepee. During the summer prior to the pilgrimage that it was constructed—and I never knew that it was going to be constructed—I was out hunting and I had this vision or this dream where I walked into this building constructed like a teepee at Lac Ste. Anne.

One of the priests, a holy priest that had passed away, Father Meriman, was there giving confession and heard my confession. Before going out, I saw some people there at the pilgrimage. Father Meriman was a holy priest that served in our area and especially around Assumption, the Dene people. ... I was given something spiritual there by Father Meriman; I won't mention what it is.

When I went to the pilgrimage that summer, when I went to the grounds, I saw this structure. Then it just hit me, and I said "Oh, God," I thought to myself, "that is exactly the way I dreamed about this building." I walked in there and everything was exactly the way I had that vision. So I knew that is wasn't a coincidence. In this situation, it was the first time I would have seen it. I saw it in my vision first and I saw this priest that had passed away giving confessions at this building.

Those are the kinds of things that a lot of Native people rely on. They know that those things just don't happen, that something is trying to tell you to do something. It is a clear indication that there's another power out there. There are things that happen that are not coincidence because there's a spiritual guidance all around us.[34]

LEGENDS

The legends of the lake are numerous. Every year, people repeat the stories of seeing extraordinary things on the lake: from sightings of St. Anne, said to have emerged on the water and to have left her footprints on a rock, to Native visions and dreams.

Francis Alexis, a band councilor and student of Alexis First Nations history, estimates that his people first arrived at the lake in the early nineteenth century, moving north from what is now North Dakota and South Dakota:

Our great, great grandfather was a young man. He had a dream about a lake. It had life in abundance. There were a lot of berries and a lot of animals. But there was something about this lake that bothered him about this dream, and he went to the old people and the old people said you have to go out and search for that dream and find it.

At that time I guess, our people were scared. They did not want to be kept like the black people who were made slaves. There were not too many of our people left and there were a lot of little kids around that were orphans. Their parents either were killed or they died in some massacre. After many years of fighting, there were not too many men.

I guess it was at this time, our grandfather had a dream and the old people told him to take these orphans. So he gathered a whole bunch of orphans together and he searched for the lake. He went to a lake north of here, went around it, but it wasn't the lake he saw in his dream. So he went looking south. I guess they looked for three years. They camped at Lake Isle, which wasn't it. While they were camped there, he went looking and he came upon Wabamun. He went around it; it wasn't the lake that he dreamt about.

So on his way back, he came here and camped. Early in the morning, they say just before sunrise, a morning star came up and my grandfather heard singing. He got up and he listened and said this is one of our songs.

Our people used to sing that song a long time ago. He listened, and as soon as he got his things ready, he started heading that way. As he got closer, the song kept getting louder and louder. Pretty soon he came by the shore of this lake. The singing was coming from the lake. He got some logs together and he built a raft, and he went to the rock island, where the singing was coming from. There was singing but when he looked around, there was nobody. There were just a whole bunch of rocks.

Our grandfather looked around and something clicked, "I seen this place before," he said. "This is the lake I saw in my dream. This is where our people will have life." He named it "Wakãmne," meaning a holy lake. I guess he pulled out his pipe, they say, and he prayed. After he prayed, he came back and put his raft on the shore and he looked towards the rock. The singing was starting to go faint and he saw a lady walking on the water. She had a hide coat; it was not tan but it was white. It had shells on it and porcupine stuff decorated on it and she had a bundle. It was a lady walking on the water. The woman spirit that represents Mother Earth, like a mother provides for us everything we need. Not only for us but also the animals and the birds; all the living things. Our people still sing songs about it at sun dance.

The singing disappeared after that. While he was walking around, he saw a whole bunch of berries. He looked at the ground and he saw that the ground can produce a lot of strawberries. Also, there was an abundance of animals—ducks, beavers, and fish. Everything they needed to depend on was there. He went back and got his people.[35]

Helen Letendre also knows the story of the drums and singing at the rock island, told to her by her grandmother. She has missed few pilgrimages since childhood:

I guess ever since a long time ago, my grandmother did not tell me when, but they used to have pilgrimages, not very many people at that time, but it started from there. When the missions came, they blessed that lake, and those drums left. There's nobody singing there anymore. She used to think that it was small men, she said, little dwarfs, that were on that rock island. She used to tell me that the lake itself is holy and when people try to do something wrong, something happens to them. People drown in the lake.[36]

The "little people" story at Lac Ste. Anne is well known among the Alexis First Nations people. These little people are considered to be custodians of the land. In the Native way, there is a great respect for all things provided for by the Creator. Everything has a spirit, and when you take a branch off a tree, you leave an offering of tobacco and thank the Creator for providing all things necessary to sustain life. It is said that when the little people come around and they find that a branch has been broken, they look for tobacco. If they do not find it, they know that something is wrong, that due respect has not been given.[37]

The oldest living elder of the Alexis First Nations, Adam Rain, was born just nine years after the the first pilgrimage began in 1889. His granddaughter Cecile Potts translates his words from the Stoney language:

The little people still exist, they come out at night, and they will always remain there for life's existence. He said people when they first came here heard singing. They used to go there and gather; it was a healing place for them. They got strength and guidance. Ask The Creator for guidance. It was a sacred place at first when all those little people were around.

He also states that there was music and drumming but when the White man came, once they blessed that lake, the singing and drumming were gone. But he said those little people still exist. He says people say there is nothing there but he says there is something there. He can feel it when he goes there. He knows and believes there are still little people there. He said it will always remain a sacred ground for the Natives because of that legend. He says some of the facts he is stating were carried on from his ancestors. They go there to pray for strength and guidance from the time they are small to the time they grow up. The little people are still in the water and when the times comes of the blessing of the lake they are there helping people heal, and one person or a couple of people will be fortunate to walk out of there healed.[38]

Another elder from the Alexis First Nations, Jean Alexis, recalled a similar story about the lake's history:

One thing I know about the lake is there was a rock island. Indians from here hear drums going there and every time they try and go there, a big wind will come and they never make it. One person believes that he seen some little people there, but if you get really close to them they would be gone. But they do not have suitable boats to go and see. When they blessed the lake, that is when the drumming stopped and people could go to the island. Anybody could go there now.[39]

BIRTH OF THE PILGRIMAGE

Not long after the mission at Lac Ste. Anne was first established in 1843, difficult times were imposed on Native people. Buffalo herds that once thundered across the plains had dwindled in numbers. The Plains Indians' entire culture was based on the buffalo, and its eventual disappearance was devastating to their way of life. The "Black Robes" are said to have foreseen this disappearance of the buffalo,[40] and this loss was viewed somewhat positively by the missionaries, including the founder of the Lac Ste. Anne Mission,

Father Thibault. During his first visit to Fort Edmonton, Thibault wrote, "When the last buffalo is dead, it will be possible to attempt something on the prairies."[41]

A calculated effort by the church and government to "change the life habits of Indians and Métis from the hunters' nomadic style to that of the farmers' sedentary one,"[42] was undertaken. But farming at Lac Ste. Anne was not working out. The poor soil and thickly wooded area around the lake were not well suited for farming or raising livestock. Early frosts and slow-maturing wheat added to the problem. The once-plentiful whitefish were now harder to come by. The community "was doomed to fail over the years."[43]

By the 1860s the mission at Lac Ste. Anne was losing its congregation and the building was deteriorating. Many people migrated to a new mission in St. Albert, which became a major agriculture centre.[44] In 1887, the church building at Lac Ste. Anne collapsed. Closing down the mission seemed to be the consensus of the Bishop and the other priests, including Father Jean-Marie Lestanc, a parish priest in St. Albert.

The decision had not been final when Father Lestanc left for an Oblates Conference in Europe, his first trip back to France since arriving to serve in western Canada some thirty years earlier. He visited his birthplace, Ste. Anne d' Auray in Brittany, France, an important pilgrimage site in Brittany.[45]

He decided to pay a visit to the shrine of Ste. Anne and at the moment he kissed the relic, he is said to have heard a voice say to him: "Et toi, qu'as tu fait pour moi?" [And you, what have you done for me?] He interpreted this to mean that he was to continue the mission at Lac Ste. Anne as well as extend devotion to Ste. Anne.[46]

When he returned to Canada, he persuaded the Bishop and the other priests that a new chapel must be built to replace the fallen structure. In

1889, the first of two pilgrimages was held on June 6. There were 171 people who heard the first pilgrimage mass.[47]

At this first pilgrimage, [the people] came to "implore" Ste. Anne for "... quelques soulagement à leurs maux et peines...," that is, beseeching for relief for their pain and heartbreaks, as well as for rain, since there was a drought in that year. It seems some of their prayers were answered since rain started to pour an hour after the pilgrimage ended....[48]

Another story about the first pilgrimage was told to Chief Johnsen Sewepegaham by a respected Elder:

In talking to various people over the years one of the stories comes to mind; I am not sure what year this would be, probably the first year they had a pilgrimage there.

The whole country was in drought. There was no rain, for months I guess, and there were different spiritual people who tried different things to have rain and it did not rain.

Until this Brother got people together and asked them to pray to St. Anne, to intercede for them, to ask for rain because the country was too dry and naturally a lot of things were suffering. People already had crops in those days and that would be affected.

The story goes that people gathered there, as many people as got word that there was going to be a prayer service to St. Anne, so she could intercede for the people to have rain. Coming out of the church they said it started raining. They didn't say how long but the rain came. For them, that was a clear sign that saints have a purpose. These were Native people who were gathered there who were asked to pray to this saint which is St. Anne. When this elder was telling me about it, different ceremonies had been tried until people went back to the simple prayer and then rain came.

This was nothing against other ceremonies, it was God's way of telling the people that prayer also could serve the same purpose. Probably talking to some Native people they would be reluctant to talk about that, but this Elder was really open to me and that is the way it was told to me and I have always believed that story.[49]

Through his granddaughter Cecile Potts, Alexis First Nations Elder Adam Rain tells a story passed on to him:

A hundred years ago there was fire around the lake. It burned for two months, all around the lake. People that were there that gathered around, prayed for that two months. Four days in a row it rained and it put that fire out. They were praying to God for him to give them guidance and protect them from this. So when it rained they said he is with us, and he will be with us, guiding us when we go to this lake.[50]

A second pilgrimage took place in 1889, on July 26, the Feast of St. Anne, a tradition that continues to this day.

Father Zéphirin Lizée, who served at the mission at the turn of the century, said the pilgrimage at Lac Ste. Anne had two purposes, one spiritual and the other social:

After the disappearance of the buffalo herds, Lac Ste. Anne's role as a gathering place for hunters and their families also vanished. With this lost role went the festive activities and the religious dedication attached to the great hunt. The pilgrimages fill this vacuum.[51]

By the turn of the century, the government was making it hard for Native people to practice their culture. The ban on performing the sun dance, introduced in 1895, was followed in 1914 by an order prohibiting Native people from appearing in their traditional clothing at fairs and stampedes.

But instead of disappearing as government officials had hoped, the rituals were moved underground and continued to be performed.[52]

The social aspect of the pilgrimage took on new importance because government authorities had introduced a pass system in 1882, making it illegal for Native people to leave their reserves without first getting permission. Gatherings such as the one at Lac Ste. Anne made it possible to see old friends and relatives.

Doreen Spence, president of the Plains Indian Cultural Survival School in Calgary, was a little girl in the last years before the pass system was abolished in 1941:

> I could see my grandparents as being there not so much to be supportive of Catholicism, but more in terms of being allowed out, the freedom of even going there because these were the days when we were not allowed off of the reserve. To me, we all thought it was so nice to be able to move. Like a bunch of cattle we would get in this big truck and go. It was a time of freedom, and people don't see that as a big issue. But to me as a young child, it was very, very important.
>
> You saw family and you were related to a lot of people. Dad would say this is your cousin from Hobbema and this one's from the Alexis and this was my so-and-so's cousin, and you were related. An extended family became a really big thing. You went back to the controlled environment and you could always look forward to something. It's very vivid in my mind and I'm so happy that my children can move freely.[53]

MODERN PILGRIMAGE

The modern pilgrimage to Lac Ste. Anne has changed in many ways from the early years. Some say the pilgrimage has become too commercialized. The gift shop sells an array of religious paraphernalia, and just a few yards east of the official church grounds is an area that has become known as "the mall," where a variety of merchants set up wood stalls offering everything from second-hand clothes to fresh bannock.

The number of people attending has kept growing. No official attendance records are kept, but RCMP estimated between 25,000 and 30,000 people came to the water in 1993.[54] Traditional Native rituals such as the drum dance, once banned by the priests, have been added to the official schedule of the pilgrimage in recent years.

But many who come to the lake do so for the same reasons people have always come here. They bring to the water their faith and hope, looking to purify and cleanse themselves. They arrive seeking a spiritual connection with traditional ways of the past. They come to express their devotion to the grandmother of Jesus.

Harmony and good feeling emanate from this place, an attraction too powerful to resist. Lac Ste. Anne seems to call out to the hearts of the people. That call is answered by the thousands who carry on their personal pilgrimages to the healing waters.

PRAYER FOR
PURIFICATION

O sacred water, the Great Creator put you here on the earth from the very Beginning of Time to be a healer and purifier. As I understand it, you are both physical and spiritual. The worst poison, pollution, germs and diseases in the world live in, around, or near the water. The biggest, meanest, deadliest, and most vicious creatures—seen and unseen—live in and around the water. Still, the water purifies itself. So nothing can harm or hurt you because you purify yourself, protect yourself, and heal yourself. This I ask for your spirit, and I ask for your help and that you doctor me. And I give you thanks for the use of your power.[55]

NOTES

1   "Pilgrimage continues to gain popularity," *Edmonton Journal*, 25 July 1992.

2   Canadian Broadcasting Corporation Radio, Andrea Marantz's "Ideas: Troubled Waters— The Pilgrimage to Lac Ste. Anne," 4 January 1994; Patricia Mitchell and Ellie Prepas, eds., *Atlas of Alberta Lakes* (Edmonton: University of Alberta Press, 1990), p. 412.

3   Translation from the Stoney Language (Onoway, Alberta: Alexis First Nations Band Office, 1995).

4   Canadian Broadcasting Corporation Radio, Andrea Marantz's "Ideas: Troubled Waters."

5   "Calgary Magazine," *Calgary Herald*, 14 August 1988.

6   Vernon Jones, interview, Alexis First Nations Band Office, Onoway, Alberta, 3 March 1995.

7   John Webster Grant, *Moon of Wintertime—Missionaries and the Indians of Canada in Encounter since 1534* (Toronto: University of Toronto Press, 1984), p. 101.

8   "Lac Ste. Anne 'Wilderness Oasis'," *Edmonton Journal*, 27 July 1964.

9   E.O. Drouin, O.M.I., M.ED., Ph.D. Lac Ste. Anne Sakahigan (Edmonton: Editions de l'ermitage, 1973), p. 13.

10 Canadian Broadcasting Corporation Radio, Andrea Marantz's "Ideas: Troubled Waters."

11 The Oblates of Mary Immaculate is a religious order founded in the south of France in 1826. Their first venture outside France was to eastern Canada in 1841. From there they moved west on their mission to bring Catholicism to the aboriginal peoples of Canada. Today there are approximately 5,000 priests and brothers based in 45 countries. Information from a telephone interview with Father Alfred Groleau, Oblate Priest, Lac Ste. Anne, 24 March 1995.

12 Father Jacques Johnson, interview held at the Missionary Oblates offices, Edmonton, Alberta, 13 March 1995.

13 Earle Waugh, B.A., M.A., Ph.D., Professor of Religious Studies, interview held at University of Alberta, Department of Religious Studies, Edmonton, Alberta, 21 February 1995.

14 Olive Patricia Dickason, B.A., M.A., Ph.D., Professor Emeritus of History, interview held at University of Alberta Press, Edmonton, Alberta, 14 February 1995.

15 Ibid.

16 Helen Letendre, Native Elder, interview held at Alexis First Nations Band Office, Onoway, Alberta, 3 March 1995.

17 Chief Johnsen Sewepegaham, Little Red River Cree Nation, Alberta, telephone interview on 28 February 1995.

18 Veronica Morin, Native Elder, Enoch Reserve, telephone interview, March 1995.

19 Father Jacques Johnson, interview, 13 March 1995.

20 Drouin, *Lac Ste. Anne Sakahigan*, p. 89. Taken from the *Codex historicus*, Volume 1, Extracts, from page 17 on. The *Codex historicus* is a diary written originally in French by a priest appointed to record the events that effected Oblate life at the time.

21 James Medford, paramedic, interview held at the Lac Ste. Anne Pilgrimage, Lac Ste. Anne, Alberta, July 1992.

22 Canadian Broadcasting Corporation Radio, Andrea Marantz's "Ideas: Troubled Waters."

23 Chief Johnsen Sewepegaham, telephone interview, 28 February 1995.

24 Earle Waugh, interview, 21 February 1995.

25 David E. Young, B.A., B.D., M.A., Ph.D., Professor of Anthropology, interview held at University of Alberta Centre for the Cross-Cultural Study of Health and Healing, 28 February 1995.

26 Father Jacques Johnson, interview, 13 March 1995.

27 John W. Pollock, Staff Archaeologist, Northeastern Alberta Archaeological Survey of Alberta, "A Preliminary Survey of Isle Lake: Lac Ste. Anne and Adjacent Sturgeon River Basin," March 1979.

28 "Finding hope in The Healing Waters: Believers flock to Lac Ste. Anne in search of medical miracles," *Edmonton Journal*, 25 July 1994, Father Jacques Johnson quoted.

29 Earle Waugh, interview, 21 February 1995.

30 "The Sacred Circle," produced and directed by Donald K. Spence; written by Donald K. Spence and Earle Waugh. University of Alberta/Access Network 1980.

31 David E. Young, interview, 28 February 1995.

32 Medicine Grizzlybear Lake, *Native Healer: Initiation Into An Ancient Art* (Wheaton, Illinois: Quest Books, 1991), p. 29.

33 Earle Waugh, interview, 21 February 1995.

34 Chief Johnsen Sewepegaham, telephone interview, 28 February 1995.

35 Francis Alexis, Native Elder, interview held at Alexis First Nations Band Office, Onoway, Alberta, 24 March 1995.

36 Helen Letendre, interview, 3 March 1995.

37 Francis Alexis, interview, 24 March 1995.

38 Adam Rain, Native Elder, interview held at Mr. Rain's home on Alexis First Nations Reserve, Onoway, translated by his granddaughter, Cecile Potts, 3 March 1995.

39 Jean Alexis, Native Elder, Alexis First Nations Reserve, Onoway, Alberta, telephone interview on 6 March 1995.

The following appeared in the *Edmonton Journal*, 4 November, 1990.

> ARCTIC "LITTLE PEOPLE" REPORTED SIGHTED
> Tribe of tiny nomads said by legend to shun civilization.
> The legend of the little people–a tribe of about 70, meter-high warriors clothed in traditional caribou skins who tote bows and arrows–above the Arctic Circle–has resurfaced with recent sightings at the Cambridge Bay dump. …

Another story about the "little people" was related to me by Keith Peterson, Cambridge Bay, during a telephone interview on 8 March 1995.

> I guess it is a local legend up here. There have been reports over the years of little people in the area, they've been seen at the gravel pit, they've been seen in other areas of the north as well. But this particular case, in Cambridge Bay that summer, about a week earlier, there was an elderly lady said she saw a little person out at the gravel pit. About a week or so later, there was a report some guys were out at the garbage dump here, about a quarter mile out of town. Four little people had been seen. The story is that they were seen carrying a tarpaulin, between them, each one had an edge, and they're walking. These guys are at this dumpsite, they see them and so three guys decided to chase them to get a closer look. So they hopped on their motorized three wheelers, and as fast as they could race to catch these little people, the little people ran faster.

40 Drouin, *Lac Ste. Anne Sakahigan*, p. 14.
41 Grant, *Moon of Wintertime*, p. 157.
42 Drouin, *Lac Ste. Anne Sakahigan*, p. 14.
43 Drouin, *Lac Ste. Anne Sakahigan*, p. 20.
44 Grant, *Moon of Wintertime*, p. 147.
45 Canadian Broadcasting Corporation Radio, Andrea Marantz's "Ideas: Troubled Waters."

46 Alice Charland, R.N., B.A., M. Theological Studies, "First Nations and the Lac Ste. Anne Pilgrimage," Master's Thesis, Athabasca University, 1995, citing Archives, Lac Ste. Anne.
47 Drouin, *Lac Ste. Anne Sakahigan*, p. 53.
48 Charland, "First Nations and the Lac Ste. Anne Pilgrimage," citing *Codex historicus*.
49 Chief Johnsen Sewepegaham, telephone interview, 28 February 1995.
50 Adam Rain, interview translated by Cecile Potts, 3 March 1995.
51 Drouin, *Lac Ste. Anne Sakahigan*, p. 53.
52 Olive Patricia Dickason, *Canada's First Nations: A History of Founding Peoples from Earliest Times* (Toronto: McClelland & Stewart, 1994) p. 286.
53 Doreen Spence, president, Plains Indian Cultural Survival School, Calgary, Alberta, telephone interview on 7 March 1995.
54 "The Faithful are Drawn to the Healing Waters," *Edmonton Journal*, 28 July 1993.
55 Medicine Grizzlybear Lake, *Native Healer*, pp. 193-94.

THE PILGRIMAGE

MARIE AUGER

JEAN D'OR PRAIRIE

"You feel different when you come out of the water. I believe that everything in the lake comes out clean. It makes you feel clean. And if you really believe in your religion, you go in the water and you come out like you somehow changed, you leave all your troubles."

Lac Ste. Anne at dusk.

"I'm here for two years now and it has helped me better myself, make me understand myself as a person. Why I walk here is for myself, for my strength, for my sobriety as well as for the people in jail, that can't make it. It's a personal sacrifice for me."

The journey for enlightenment or spiritual power sometimes begins with a walk to the pilgrimage as a means of self sacrifice (right). The first people arrive on the grounds two weeks before the start of the ceremonies (opposite).

"It is a very special place and I think this place has a lot of powers in our own traditional, spiritual way. There are four things in our lives that have very special powers, the four directions Mother Earth provides us: water, air, shelter and the food. Those four things are powerful, you use it everyday and you believe in it. If you didn't believe in water you wouldn't drink water, right? So in the same sense it has its own powers.

"I went to a residential school and before I went to a residential school, the church that was in our community at the time was Catholic, but it was a different kind of Catholic. It wasn't very stressed to the point where it drove you insane. People that went to residential schools became very indoctrinated into the system, and we were taught that to even talk to White people was wrong. We were taught that to pray to the Great Spirit was wrong and there was such a person called Jesus.

"But by no means am I here because I am a Catholic. I am here because of my own beliefs in the earth, and I know there is something up there that has control of us. It's almost like a destiny, something that we look forward to meeting with one day. That's all it is, it's very simple. We accept everything on this earth as indigenous people of this world. In every direction you turn there's aboriginal people. To this day, there hasn't been one group of people that has ever been wiped out on this face of the Earth. That means that we are here as long as we allow ourselves to be here, so there is no splitting up religions. Yesterday it was beautiful to share the people that came from Mexico and from Europe, to share their way that they pray, to talk to the spirit. It's that simple, we accept everyone's way. Our way is not necessarily the right way. There's only four colours in this world: It's the white, the yellow, the black and the red. When you go to our sweat lodges, those are the colours that are being used."

The beauty and grace of ritual movement join forces with a
powerful rhythm in the sacred songs of the drum dance.

23

"I think it's pretty neat, all the people coming together, it's like one big family. Myself, I have beliefs in the water. It's bringing everybody closer together. Once they start praying a lot, you believe in it, you believe in yourself, you believe in God. They don't really get sick a lot; things start going their way, making life a little easier for them. You hear a lot of that back home."

KEITH WIDOW
NORTHWEST TERRITORIES

Aerial view of the Blessing of the Lake.

C E C I L E   P O T T S
A L E X I S   N A T I O N

"It is run by Christianity but people go there to gather and meet friends. I brought my kids over there just to swim in the water. It's just like, you know, Klondike Days. ... My grandfather was saying that one time he was really sick and he walked into the water and he got better. And then he said this one time he seen this old man going inside there with crutches. When he came out that old man just threw his crutches on the side and he started walking alone. What I really would like to see is people getting healed, I have never seen it."

Thousands wade slowly and carefully into the water during the Blessing of the Lake ceremony. The lake floor is shallow but rocky and uneven in spots, making the walk difficult.

As many as 30,000 people visit the grounds during the five-day pilgrimage. Some come to watch, others come to bathe in the water seeking spiritual or physical healing.

PIERRE DZEYLION
WOLLASTON LAKE

"It helps me a lot. It's like a freedom, a release. When you take off from this place, you feel lonesome for this place. I'd like to stay here longer."

The first recorded instances of healing were noted at the first Church-sanctioned pilgrimage in 1889.

BEVERLY WHITFORD
EDMONTON

"I feel the pilgrimage brings people together for all the right reasons and I think that the Lord Himself is a good enough reason. The way families come together, it really means allot to me for my kids to know something like this. They believe in something because they don't have a religion of their own, I've never got them baptized. I want them to discover this on their own. I feel so at peace here, my worries just seem to drift away. They stay where I come from. It only lasts while I'm here, unfortunately. When I was a child I saw some healing powers of this water. There was some very troubled people when I was a little kid and it seemed to have brought all that anger and trouble out of them. I remember that as a child. I was ten years old. The memory stayed with me and I think that was kind of a sign to bring my kids back. There's probably ten times more people here now then when I was a child, and I think that's so beautiful. Because we need something else besides each other."

A woman laughs in the water during the Blessing of the Lake ceremony.

The once pure, clear water is now murky. But the stories of healing that circulate around the pilgrimage camp still reinforce the waters' promise of curative powers.

"All spiritualities come from the same spring, and all the spiritualities anywhere in the world are linked together."

Water is a powerful symbol in Native culture: the fourth power of creation, the blood of the land. In Catholicism, water blessed by the priest becomes holy water used to cleanse and baptize.

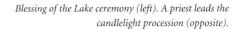
Blessing of the Lake ceremony (left). A priest leads the candlelight procession (opposite).

WILSON GAUCHER
GRANDE CACHE

"People have been gathering here for many years to worship with old buddies that you hardly see. Different denominations come here, not only the Catholic people. We know there's only one God."

"I think it's the gathering of the people, all peoples of all nations that put the power within the water to heal themselves, spiritually, mentally, emotionally, physically. I think it's just the people themselves that have the power within and they go to a place like this to find it."

People wait patiently in line for blessings from healers as well as priests.

Inside the shrine, a woman has fainted during an intense encounter with a healer (opposite).

JEAN ALEXIS
ALEXIS NATION

"We have that shrine. There was lots of canes and crutches that hang there. I guess crippled people would go there with canes and stuff and they walk out. They forgot their canes. They used to be all hanging there, and that was the miracles I guess. I don't know if we still see miracles like that now, but if you go to the shrine, those things are still hanging there."

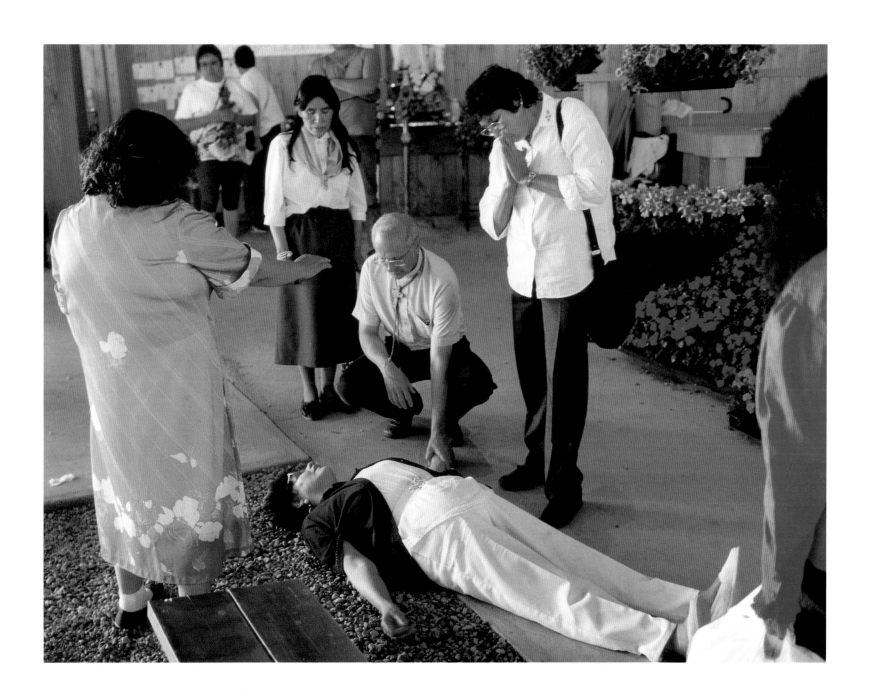

Many healers with no affiliation to the Church come to the pilgrimage to bless the sick.

FLORENCE LARGE
SADDLE LAKE

"I think what the lake symbolizes to me is faith, the faith that people have, the miracles that have happened that have not been told. I'm sure that people have been healed from here that the world does not know of. When I think back to my childhood, my Grandfather and Grandmother really believed in coming here every year. Somehow along the way, to me it lost the reverence. It has almost become too commercialized. We were taught to respect the lake."

46

ANGELINA ANORE
WINNIPEG

"It's a very, very, special place. The young now don't know where they're going, so we have to pray hard for them. They are like plants growing. We are neglecting some of them now, we have to love and care for them. I know if you have faith, you're going to heal. Go here and believe, I tell you, you're going to heal. All we have to do is pray. I'm not just coming here to pray for my family—I pray for all the entire world."

The outdoor Stations of the Cross provide a setting in which to consult with priests and pray.

Religious icons are placed throughout the grounds (opposite). Members of the congregation are reflected in the photograph of a priest on the wall inside the shrine (left).

"It's a healing place. It's the water. It's the mass. I come here every year to pray for healing, pray for family. It works. I notice the changes in people."

GRACE METCHAWAIS
COLD LAKE

For some people, prayers begin at dawn, continuing throughout the day and well into the night. Candlelight procession (right); statue of St. Anne (opposite).

St. Anne is significant to many Native people as the grandmother of Jesus,
since the grandmother is a highly respected and important figure in
Native culture. A woman prays by the statue of St. Anne.

EMILY CUMMINGS
BUFFALO NARROWS

"I pray for my kids most. It's the boys, they take drugs and alcohol, but I don't give up, I light the candles for them in the church. That's all I could do. When I first came here, I went in the water—just like you weren't even touching the ground, just like you were kinda floating in the water. That's what makes me come back every year."

*The pilgrimage is also a social place, a chance to meet with old
friends (left). Young men relax at one of the outdoor
Stations of the Cross (opposite).*

JOHN STARR
SLAVE LAKE

"Younger people are starting to learn about what's happening here. When
you come here you relax, you pray. Meet your friends, friends you haven't
seen, and this is the best place to meet your friends that you haven't seen
for years."

56

DESMOND RAIN
EDMONTON

"My dad died about a year ago, so I figure I'd say a little prayer for him. I never had a chance to do much for him when he was alive. I figure I'd do this at least."

The cemetery at Lac Ste. Anne is a short walk from the shrine.

AUGUSTANA UNIVERSITY COLLEGE
LIBRARY

The history of this lake goes back long before the arrival of the missionaries in 1843. It was a traditional summer gathering place for Native people. The Cree name for the lake is Manito Sakahigan or "Lake of the Spirit."

Water is collected in jars, gas containers, water jugs and pop bottles to be used against ailments year 'round and given to those who could not make the trip.

VICTOR LETENDRE
LAC STE. ANNE

"That water was pure then, cold, clear water. I used to throw a can down and measure the depth of the water, dive down and bring it back up. One thing I'll always remember that I used to fish with my dad on that lake when I was young, and he never let me throw anything in the lake, never. You'll poison the water he said. ... We can't drink it now."

The campground is a colourful and vibrant place, dotted with tents and teepees. At the end of the week, a convoy of buses, trucks and cars travel down the dirt and gravel road on their way back home.

"I got drowsy during the day and fell asleep. In my sleep I can see the lake and it is good, but over there where the sun rises and over there where the sun goes down, these rainbows appeared. I was being called to look at them. I stood up and looked at them. Under these rainbows it almost looked as if the leaves were green and yellow. Under one of the rainbows in a muddy kind of water I see a person but I can't seem to see the person too clearly. I was being told in my dream, 'You will look at it again; the next time you will know more about the situation.'

"I woke up, I stood up and told my sons by the campfire there. I said to them, 'My son, over there where you can see a full view of the lake, that's where I had been taken in my dream.' I went over among the rows of houses where there is a store. I came back but still it was on my mind. I thought, I wish I could see that person again about the lake here. I had been allowed to look down upon the lake before in my dream, but here in this world, I have never see this body of water with my mortal body. Likewise, I don't know why they pray to this body of water so I thought I wanted to know, how it came to be like that.

"I went to sleep. I had not slept long when I heard a person speaking to me. The person said, 'You will have a look at the people again.' This time, nothing obscured my vision, it is right in the open. The person said, 'The first time you did not have a good look at this body of water because it was meant for this world. Now you will look upon this place as it really is.'

"I stood up and looked upon the lake. Above the lake I see something going down to my eye level which forms into a circle. Upon that people appeared one after another. I can see six persons standing upon it. Directly above, in the middle, in the open, stood a person. He held his hands like this [open arms]. He was looking around and he was standing above the level of the other six persons. I thought to myself, 'Is he the one who they call the Son of our Father? If he is, I am happy to be looking upon him.' The six persons clothing looked different. 'Why is that?', I thought to myself. 'If they were angels they will all look alike'. The person told me, 'No! The three on this side, they are the ones who work with the White people, the other three work with the Indians, that's who they are. The one in the middle above, he is the one they call the Son of our Father. He is the one who prepared this body of water you look upon for the people before your time. He prepared this when the world was still young. That is why you are seeing it.'

"It's amazing, that body of water looked beautiful. I was still looking at that middle person and it was then that the person told me to look down. Below was this body of water, there were no ripples or waves on the water. The water looked like when you first see a smooth frozen ice surface in the fall. How had He walked on this body of water? He walked straight towards the shore where His footprints are visible on the shoreline. That is where a huge stone sits. Where the big stone sits is where His footprints are visible upon the rock.

"I see a person in a canoe. I think it was a person sitting in a canoe, resting himself on a canoe paddle and he seems to be really listening. He's the one who announced the story of this place. He is a person of this place in the past."

WILLY DENECHOAN
CHATEH

Reflection in an outdoor Station of the Cross mural.

66

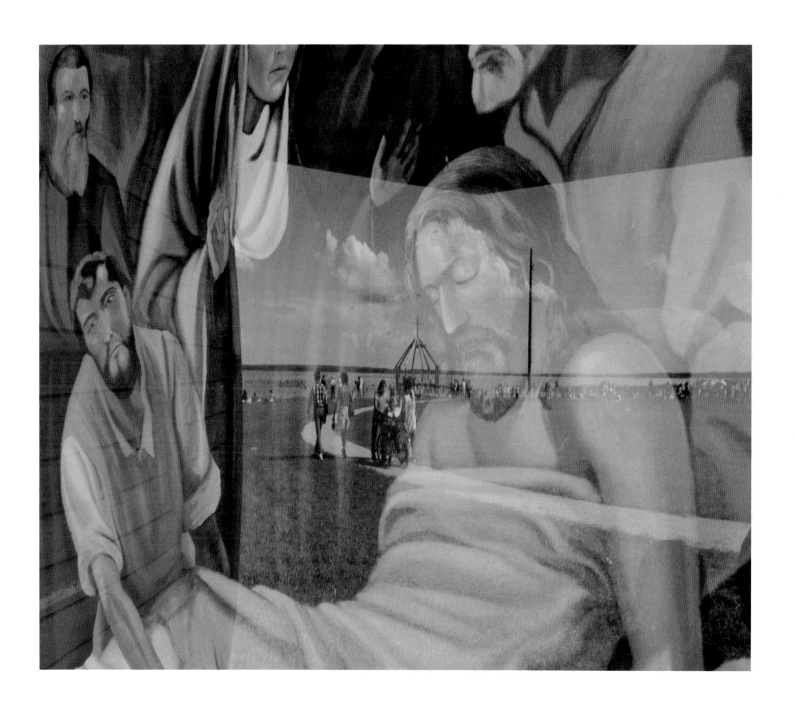

*Hundreds—sometimes thousands—of people participate in the candlelight
procession. This procession makes its way slowly past the lake.*

"I think it's the Holy Spirit feeling, everybody joining together, praising the
Lord. St. Anne is special to me because she was the one I went towards
when I was young and had problems."

DOREEN TRUDEAU
EDMONTON

PAUL BEAUREGARD
WABASCA

"I believe there has been miracles, not broadcasted you know, but kept among some of the people themselves, that miracles do happen. I know some myself, but that's not in the newspapers. I think it's the faith. … I think the Catholic Church is starting to recognize that there is a Native spirituality. It has always been there. It's not written; it's just that Indian people have always lived a very spiritual life. They have their beliefs and they have learned to live in harmony with nature and they have learned to respect nature because that's their main existence."

A time exposure records the path of fire caused by the candles in the candlelight procession.

An old Lakota man was asked how he understood the child. He answered,
"The child is a person who has just come from the Great Mysterious,
and I who am an old man am about to return to the Great Mystery.
*And so in reality we are very close to each other." ***

* Brown, Joseph Epes. *The Spiritual Legacy of the American Indian.* New York: Crossroad, 1982, p. 120.

"I am an Indian. I talk Cree. Cree mass would be fine for me but any other service is good because I believe in God. As long as you know how to pray you fit in any church. There's only one God everybody prays for."

The neon cross atop the shrine and a Native cross carved
from cedar by artist Albert Gerritsen.

LIST OF PHOTOGRAPHS

All photographs taken the last week in July.

BIBLIOGRAPHY

Babin, B.R. *Lac Sainte Anne Pilgrimage: Through the Medium of 18 Colored Photographs.* Edmonton: Missionary Oblates, 1982.

Brown, Joseph Epes. *The Spiritual Legacy of the American Indian.* New York: Crossroad, 1982.

Callihoo, Victoria. "Early Life in Lac Ste. Anne and St. Albert in the Eighteen Seventies." *Alberta Historical Review* 1(3) (November 1953): 21–26.

Charland, Alice. "First Nations and the Lac Ste. Anne Pilgrimage." Master's thesis, Athabasca University, 1995.

Davison, Vi, ed. *Spirits and Trails of Lac Ste. Anne.* Alberta Beach: Alberta Beach and District Pioneers and Archives Society, 1982.

Dickason, Olive Patricia. *Canada's First Nations: A History of Founding Peoples from Earliest Times.* Toronto: McClelland and Stewart, 1992.

Drouin, Emeric O'Neil. *Lac Ste. Anne Sakahigan.* Edmonton: Editions de L'Ermitage, 1973.

Eliade, Mircea. *Myths, Dreams & Mysteries: The Encounter between Contemporary Faiths and Archaic Reality*. Trans. Philip Mairet. London: Fontana, 1968.

Glover, Richard. *David Thompson's Narrative 1784-1812*. Toronto: Champlain Society, 1962.

Grant, John Webster. *Moon of Wintertime: Missionaries and the Indians of Canada in Encounter since 1534*. Toronto: University of Toronto Press, 1984.

Grey Nuns Archives, Edmonton.

Hultkrantz, Åke. *Native Religions of North America: The Power of Visions and Fertility*. San Francisco: Harper, 1987.

Jamieson, Col. Frederick C. "The Edmonton Hunt." *Alberta Historical Review* 1(1) (April 1953): 21-33.

Lake, Medicine Grizzlybear. *Native Healer: Initiation into an Ancient Art*. Wheaton, Illinois: Quest Books, 1991.

Marantz, Andrea. "Troubled Waters: The Pilgrimage to Lac Ste. Anne." Radio Documentary, Canadian Broadcasting Corporation, 1993.

McCarthy, Martha. *From the Great River to the Ends of the Earth: The Oblates and the Dene 1847-1921*. Edmonton: University of Alberta Press. Forthcoming.

Mitchell, Patricia and Ellie Prepas, eds. *Atlas of Alberta Lakes*. Edmonton: University of Alberta Press, 1990.

Pollock, John W. "A Preliminary Survey of Isle Lake, Lac Ste. Anne and Adjacent Sturgeon River Basin." Northeastern Alberta Archaeological Survey of Alberta, 1979.

Provincial Archives of Alberta, Edmonton.

The Sacred Circle. The Sacred Circle: Recovery. Produced and directed by Donald K. Spence. Written by Donald K. Spence and Dr. Earle Waugh. With Adrian Hope. University of Alberta/Access Network, 1980.

Silversides, Brock V. *The Face Pullers: Photographing Native Canadians 1871-1939*. Saskatoon: Fifth House, 1994.

Interviews

Eugene Alexis
Francis Alexis
Jean Alexis
Anne Anderson
Dr. Olive Dickason
Father Rene Fumoleau
Father Alfred Groleau
Father Jacques Johnson
Helen Letendre
Victor Letendre
Elizabeth Macpherson

Raven Makkinnaw
Andrea Marantz
Father Gaston Monmenier
James Medford
Veronica Morin
Dr. Michael Payne
Chief Johnsen Sewepegaham
Doreen Spence
Dr. Earle Waugh
Dr. David E. Young